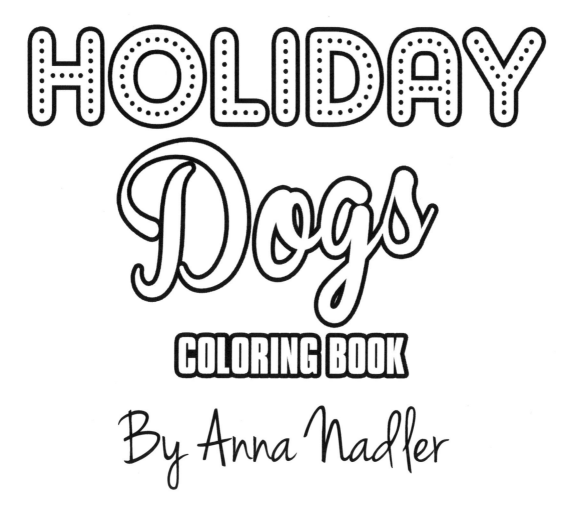

HOLIDAY Dogs
COLORING BOOK
By Anna Nadler

About the Artist

Anna Nadler is an illustrator, graphic designer and author, who lives and works in New York City. She loves drawing fashion, people, animals and architecture, as well as creating unique logo designs for various companies from around the world. You can view more of her work on her website - www.annanadler.com and on social media platforms. You can also find many of her original art books in her Amazon.com book store, where she is always adding new journals, diaries, notebooks, children's books, gift books, planners and coloring books. In her free time Anna loves traveling, singing jazz songs and spending quality time with her friends and family.

Thank you for coloring this book!
If you enjoyed it, please leave a review
on Amazon.com!

Printed in Great Britain
by Amazon